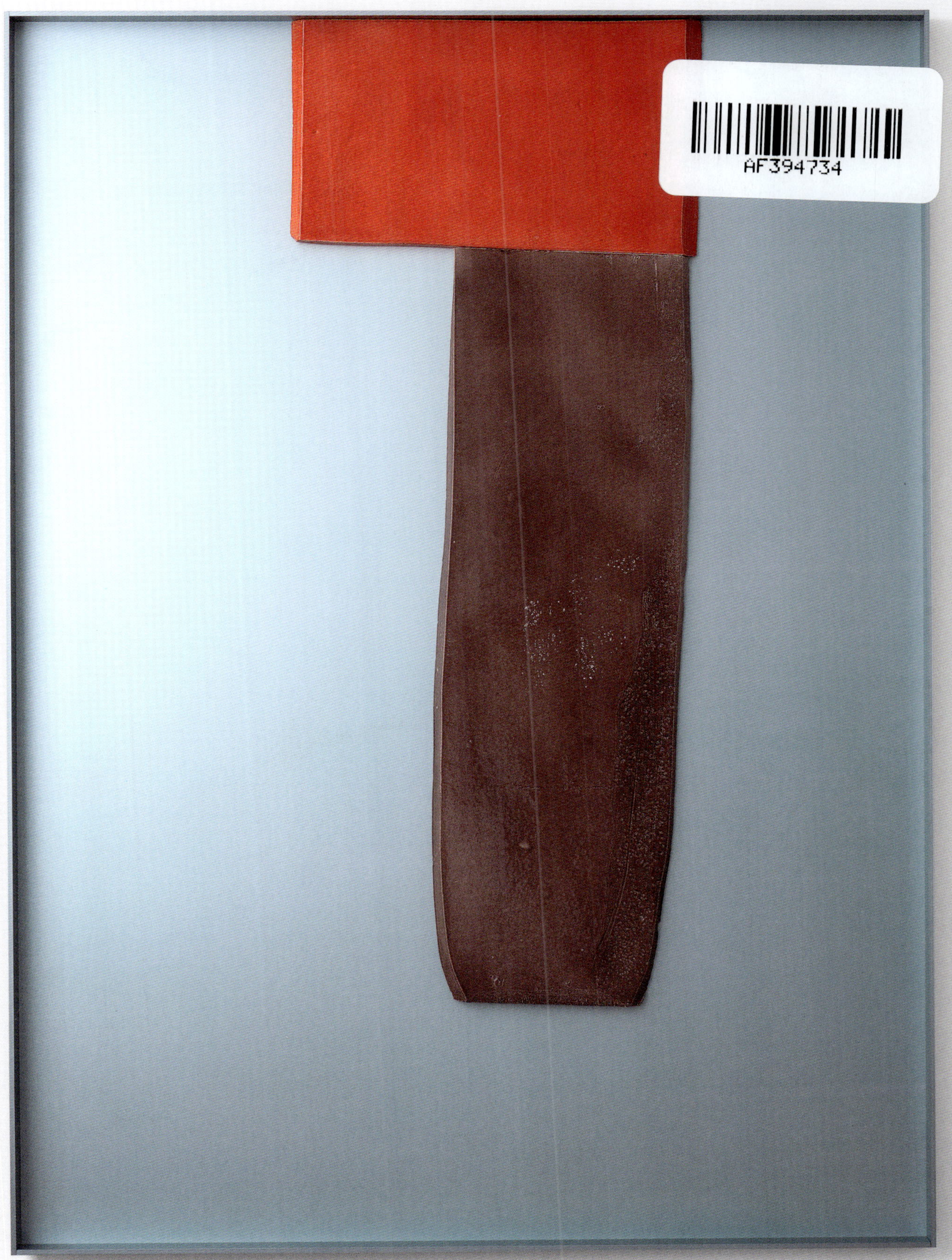

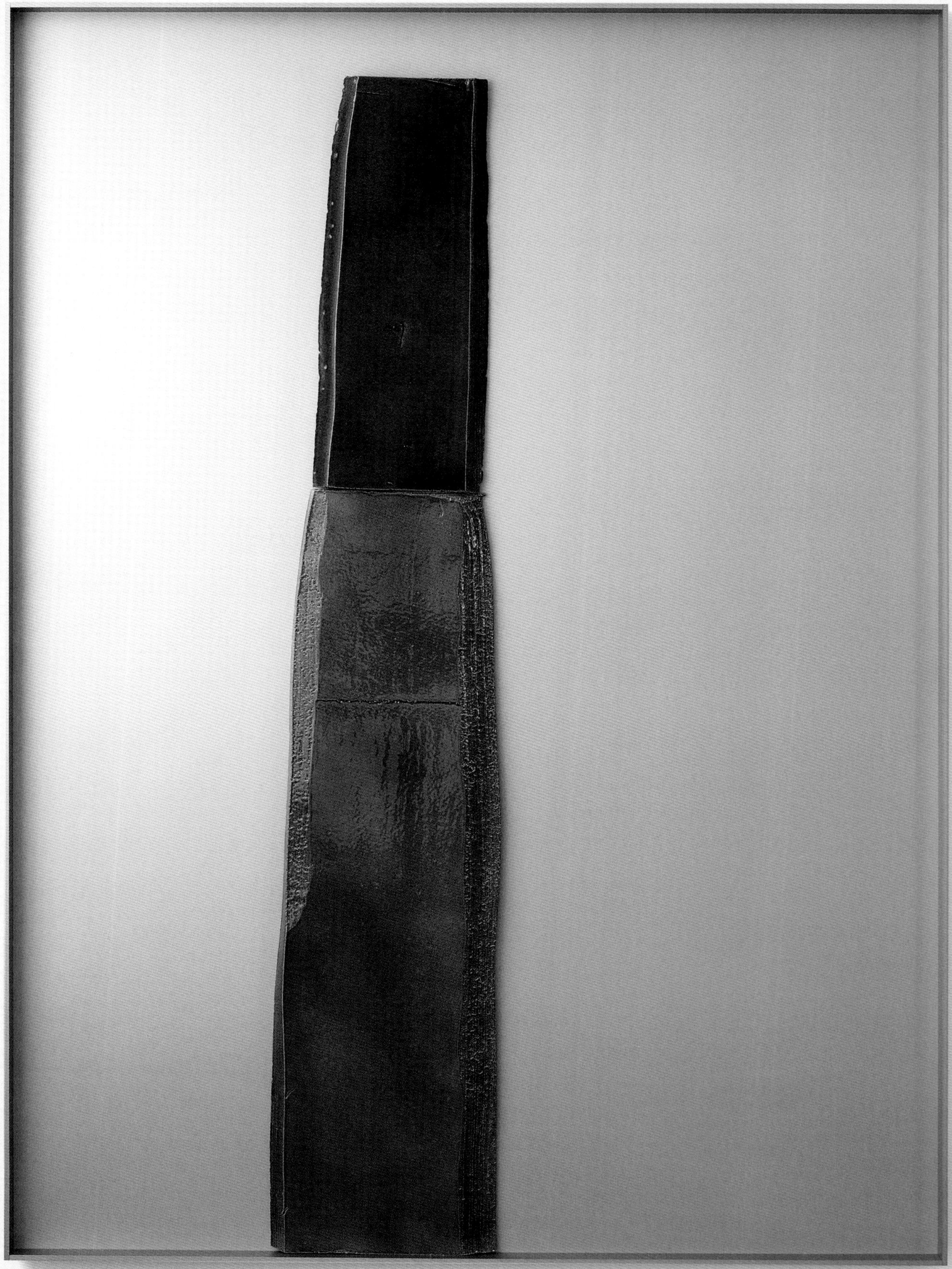

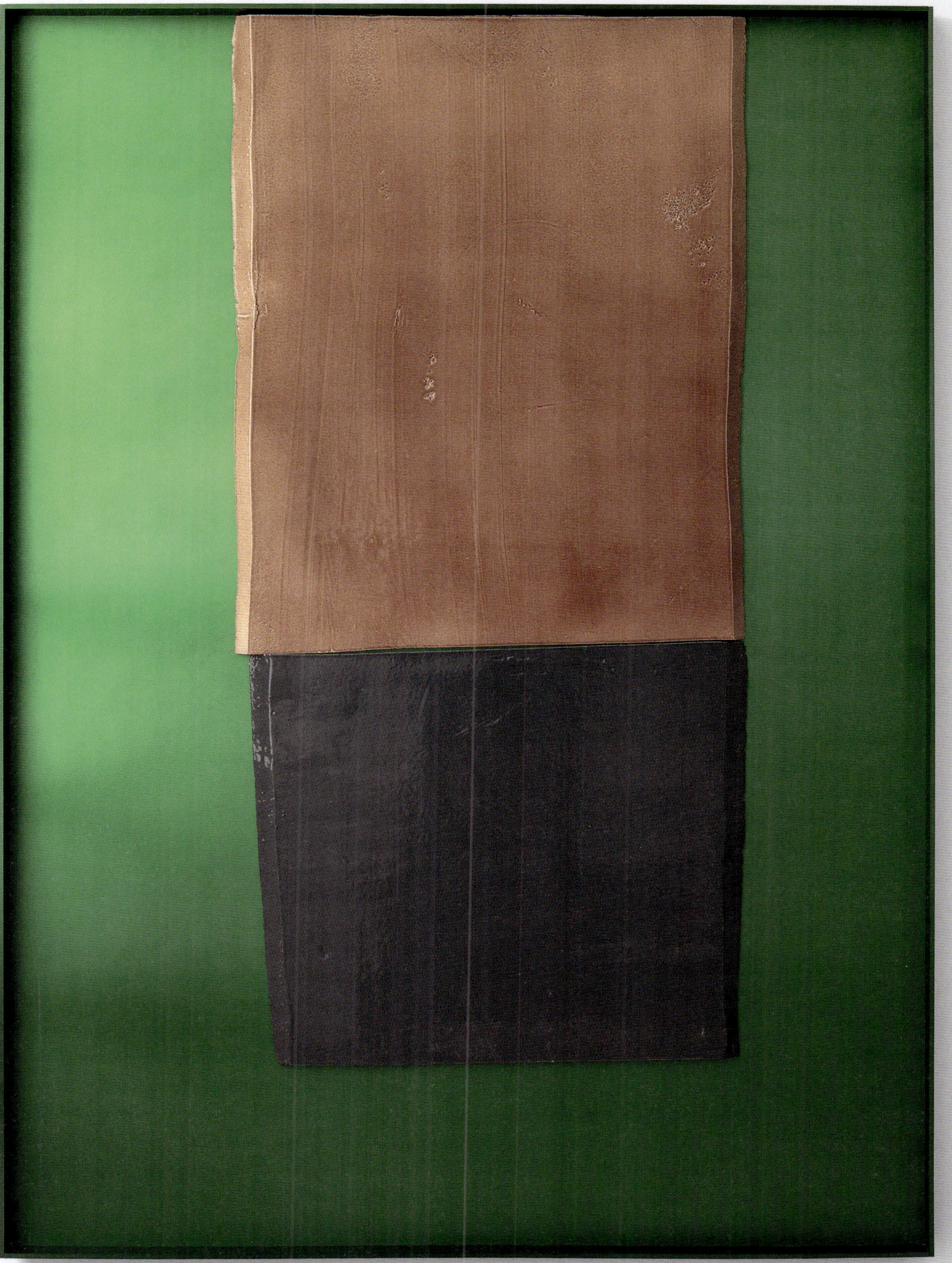

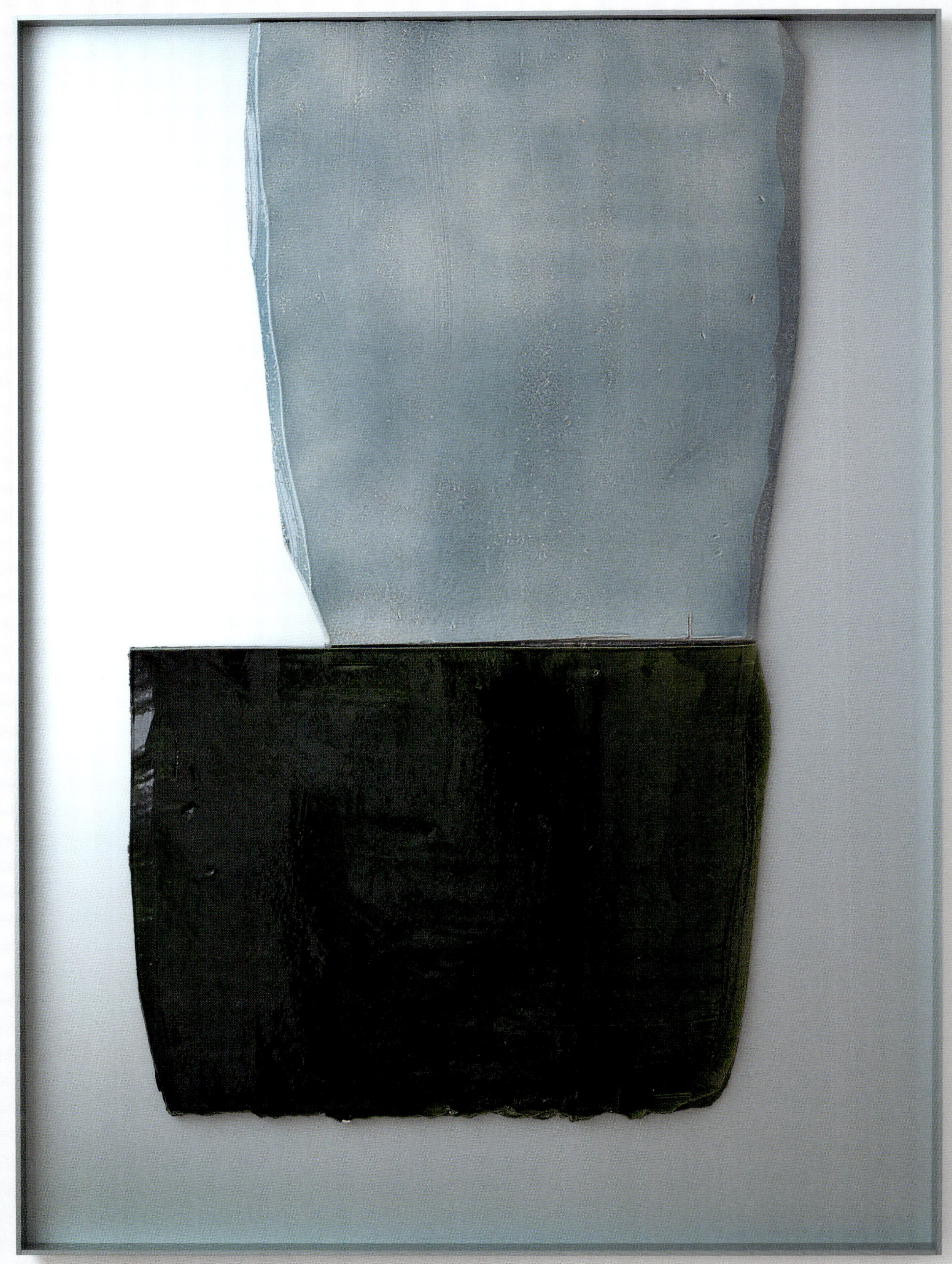

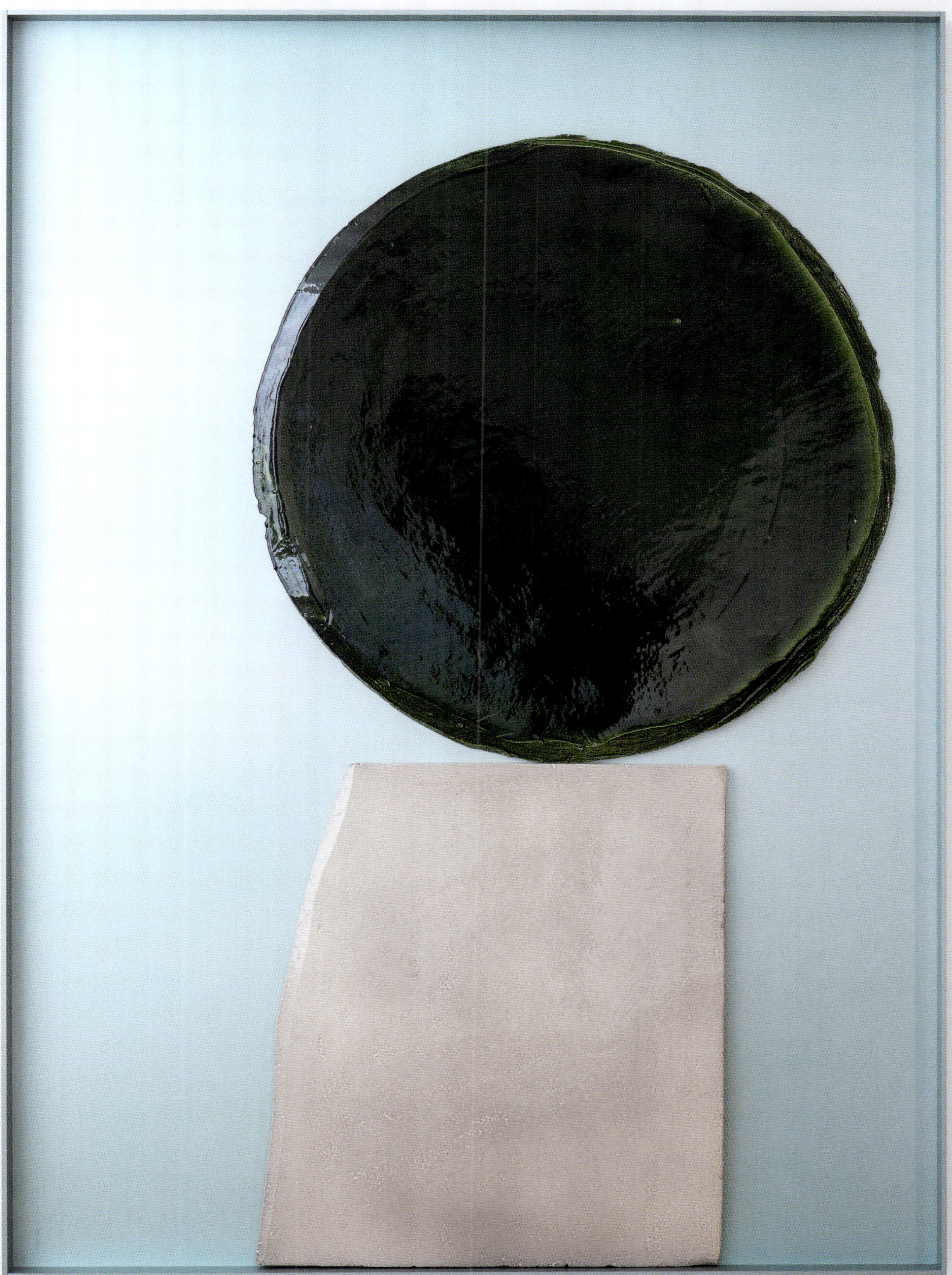

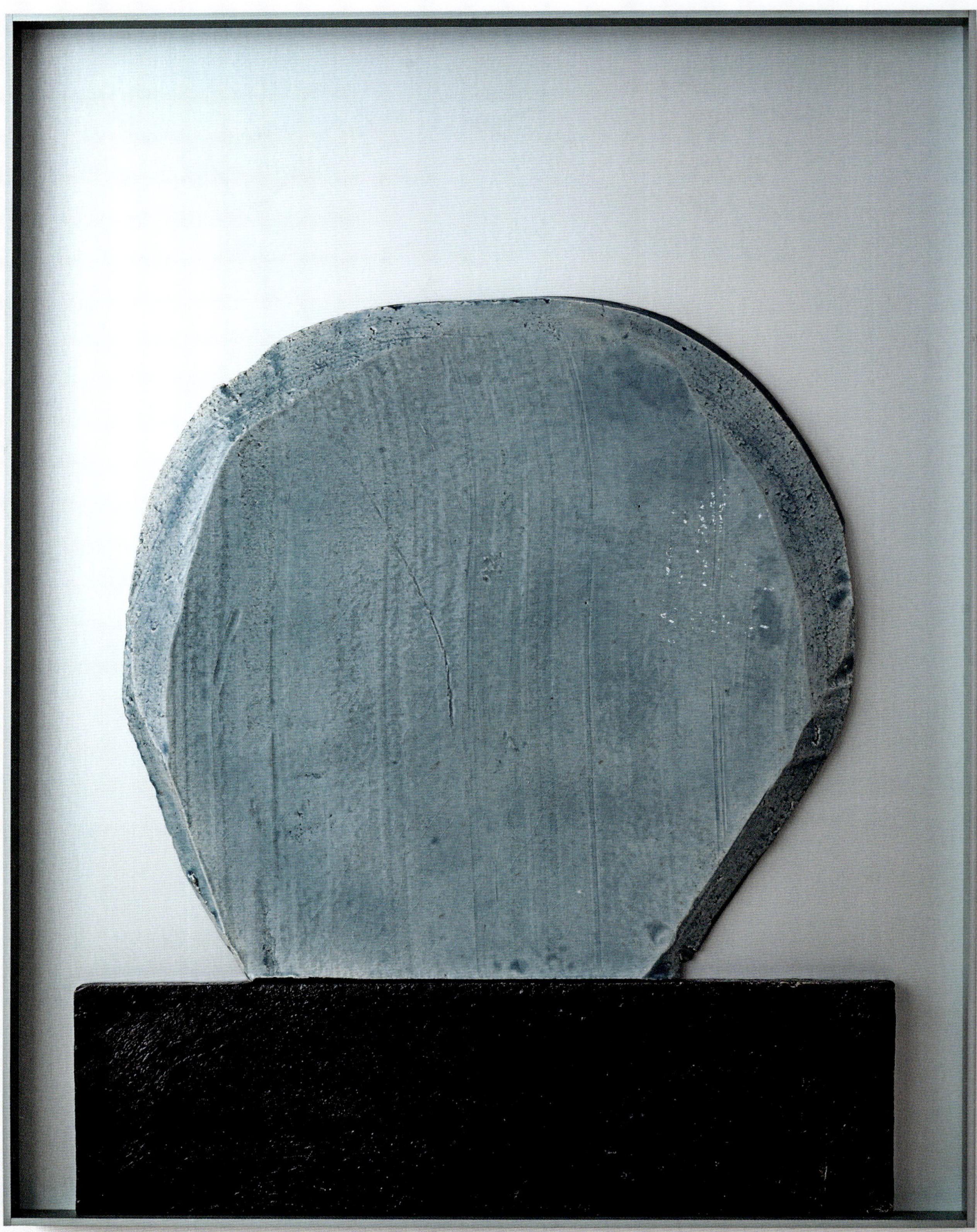

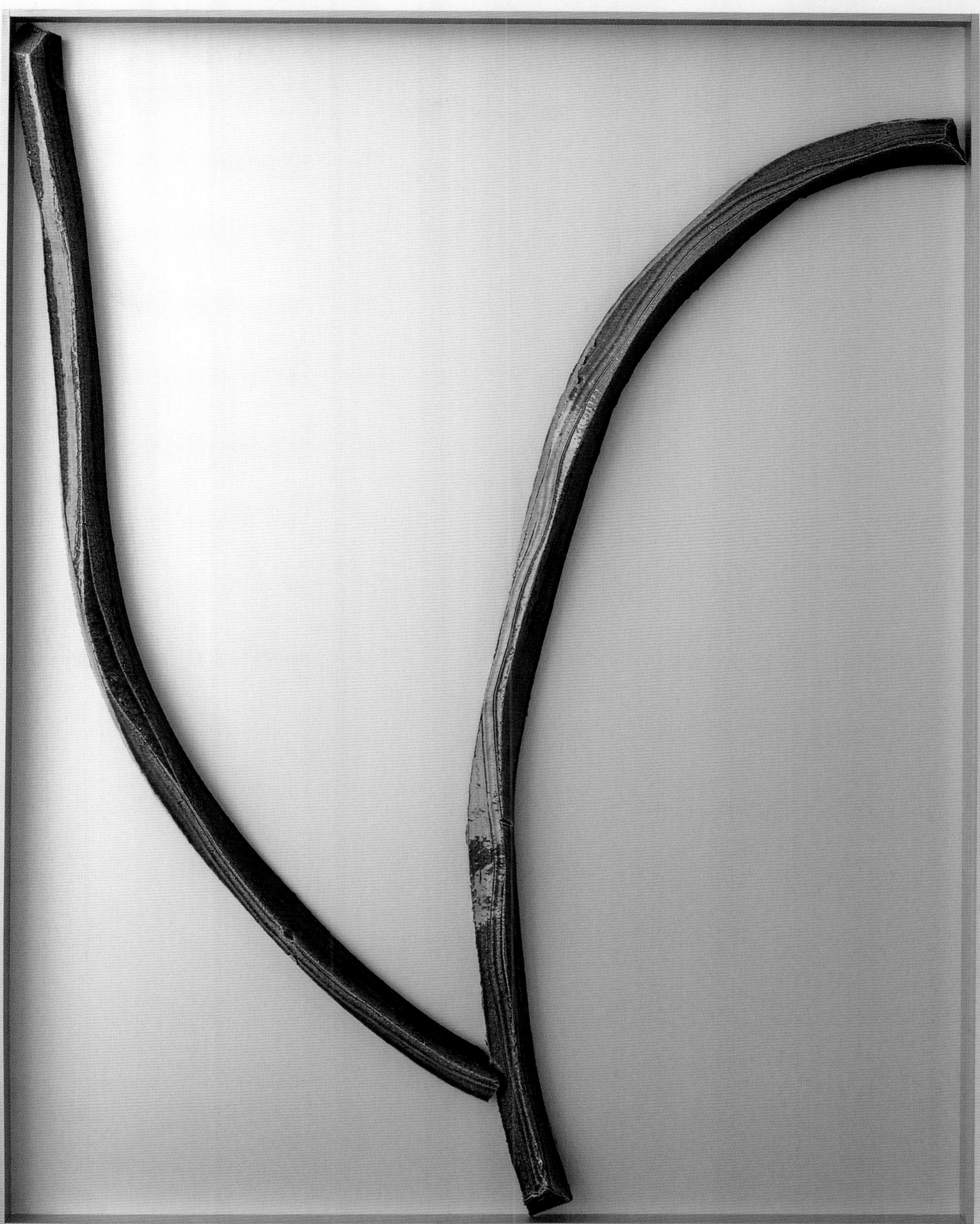

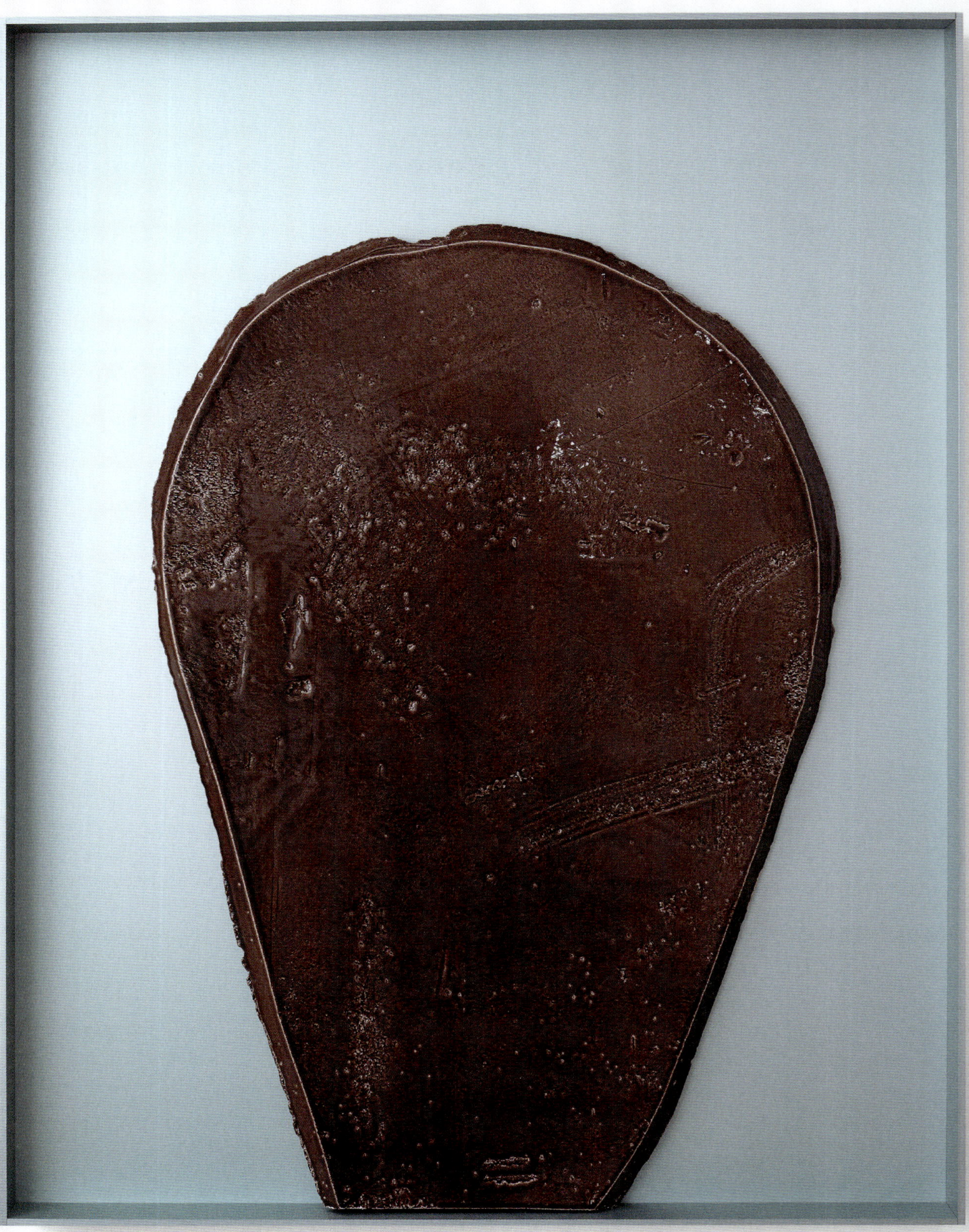

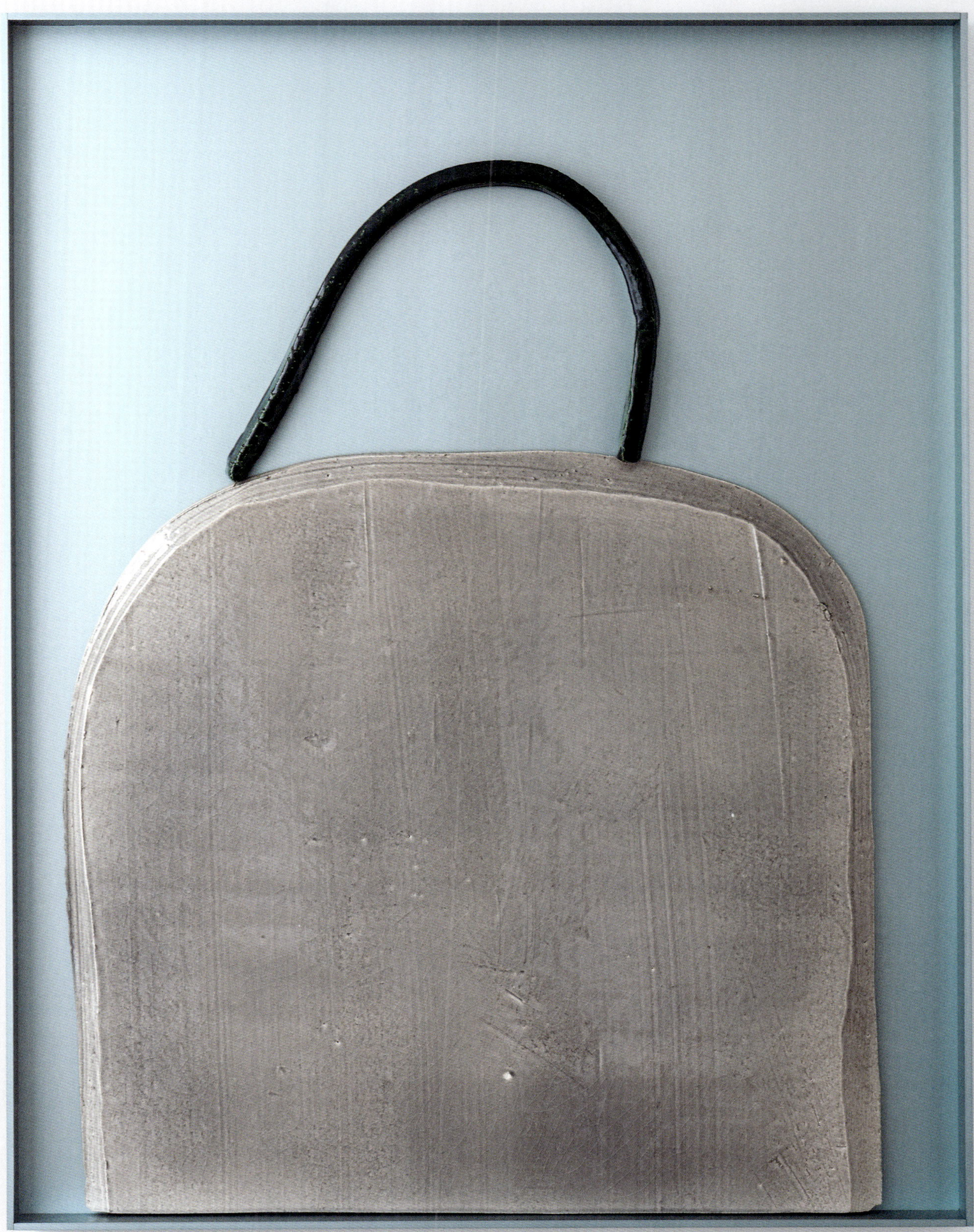

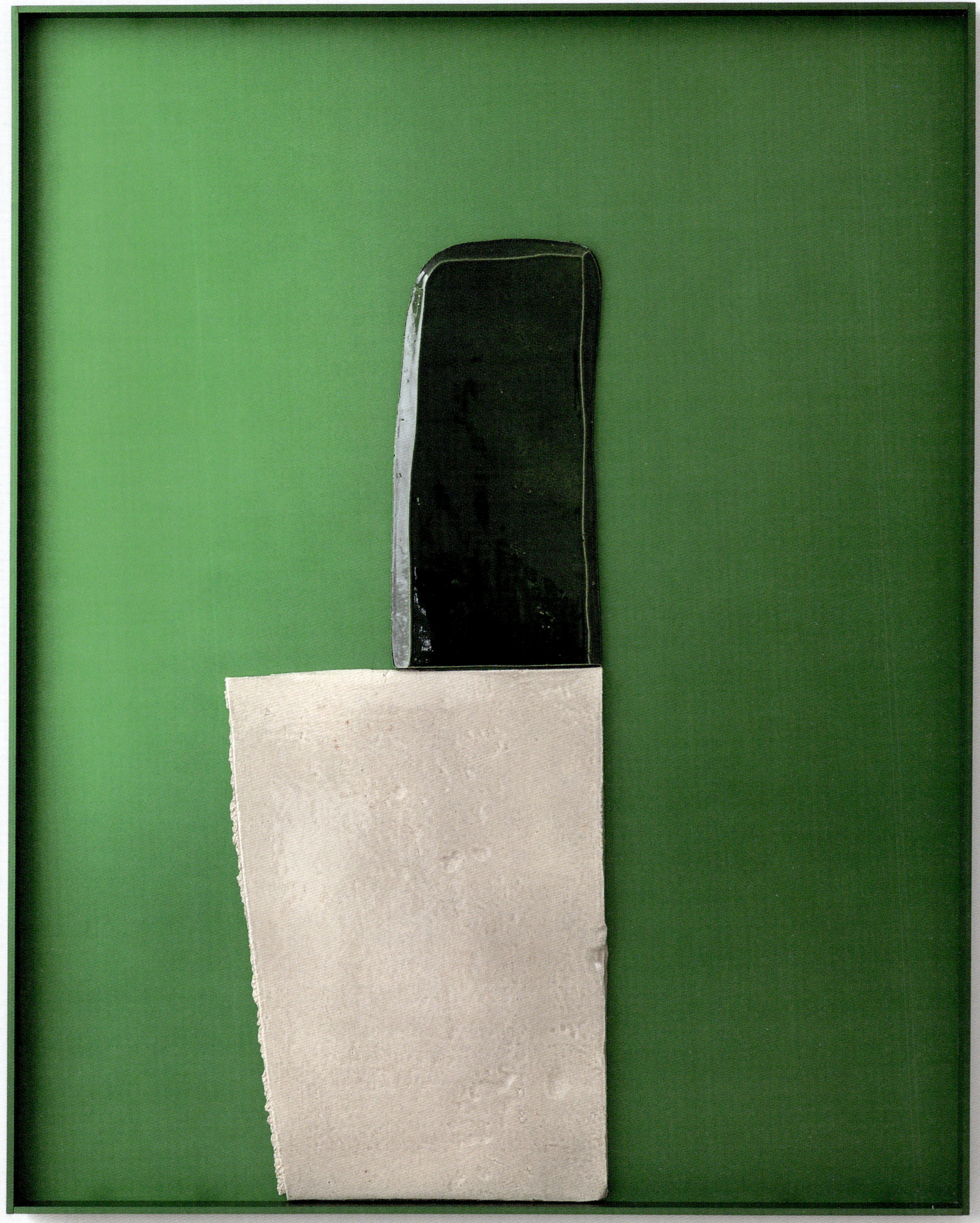

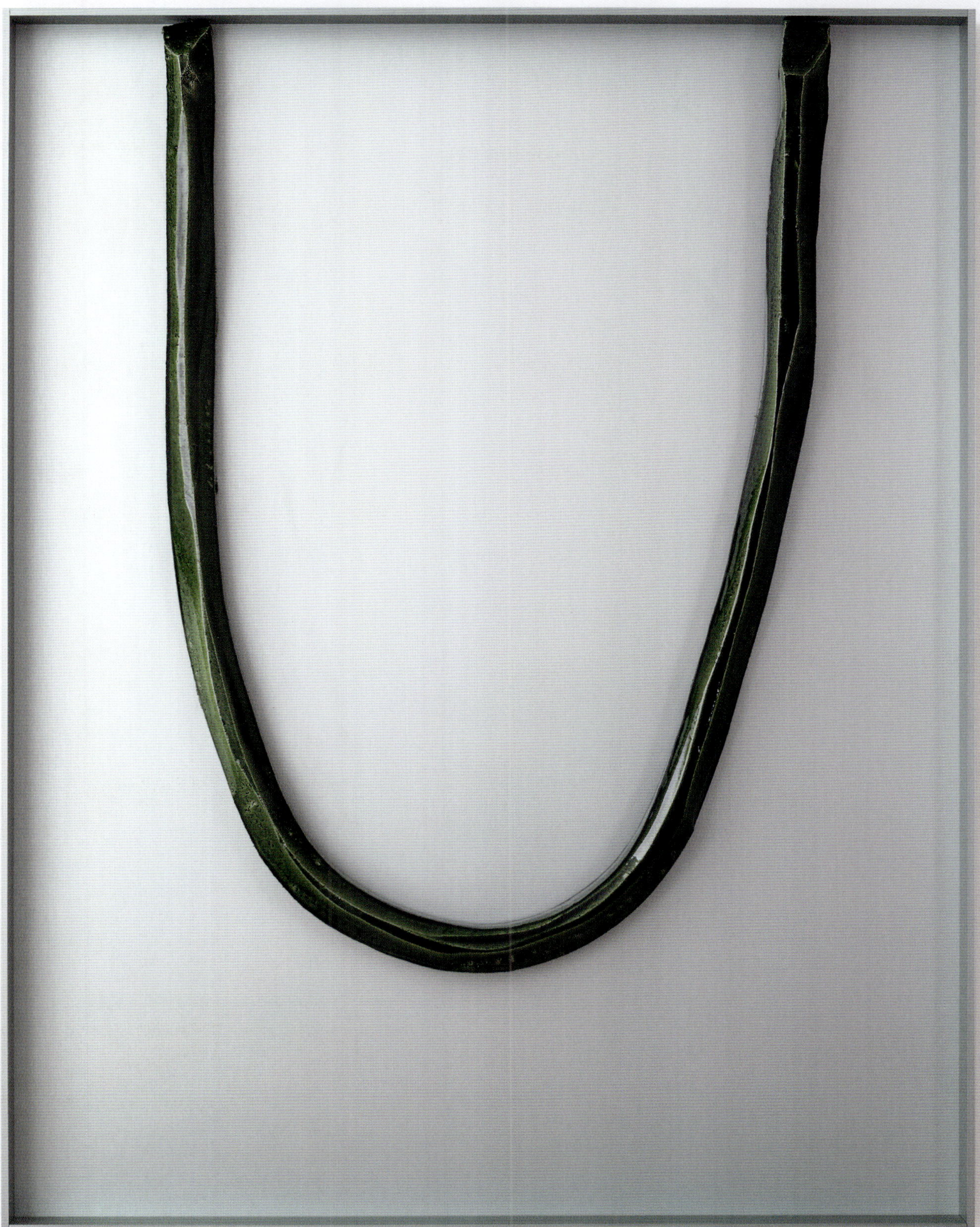

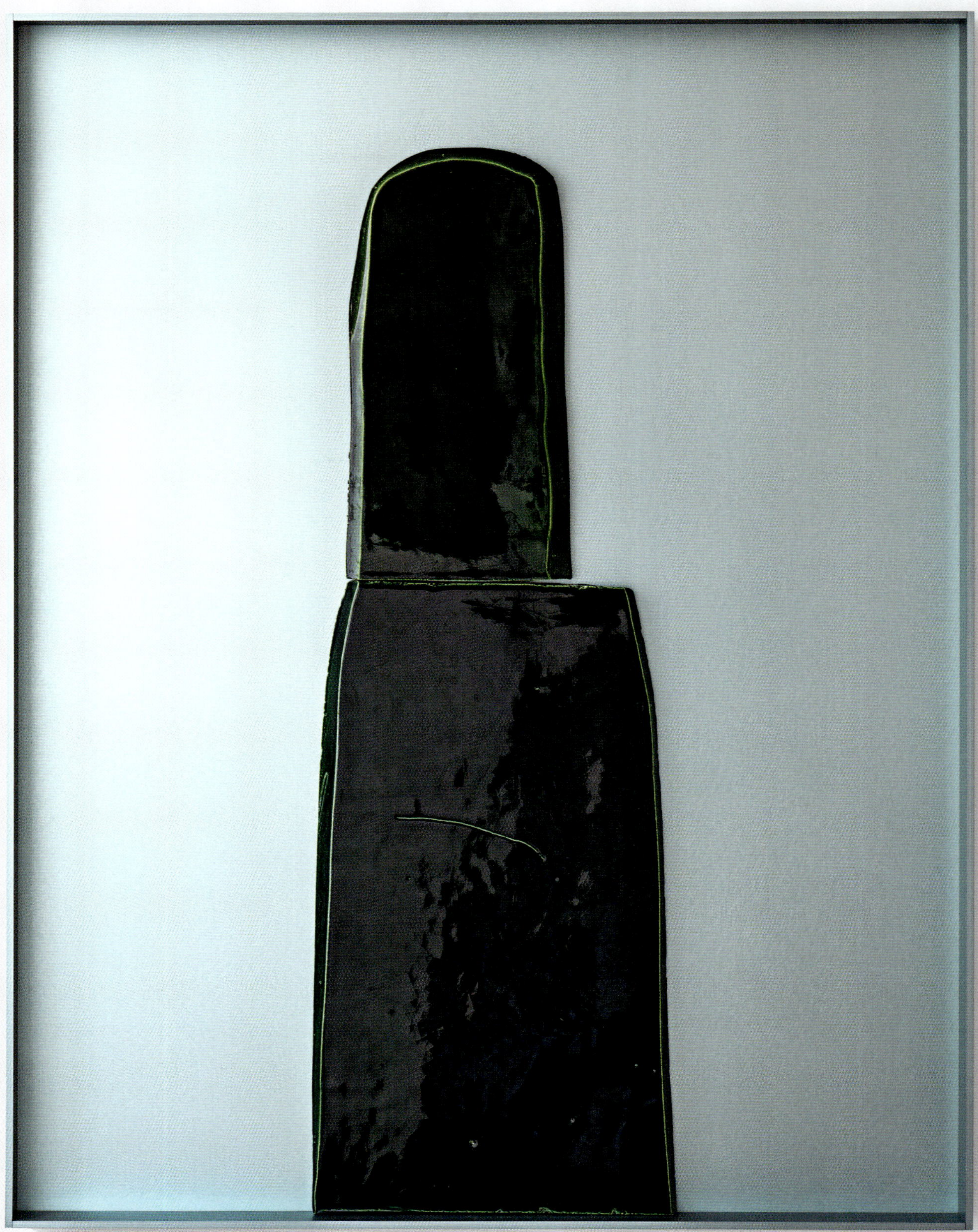

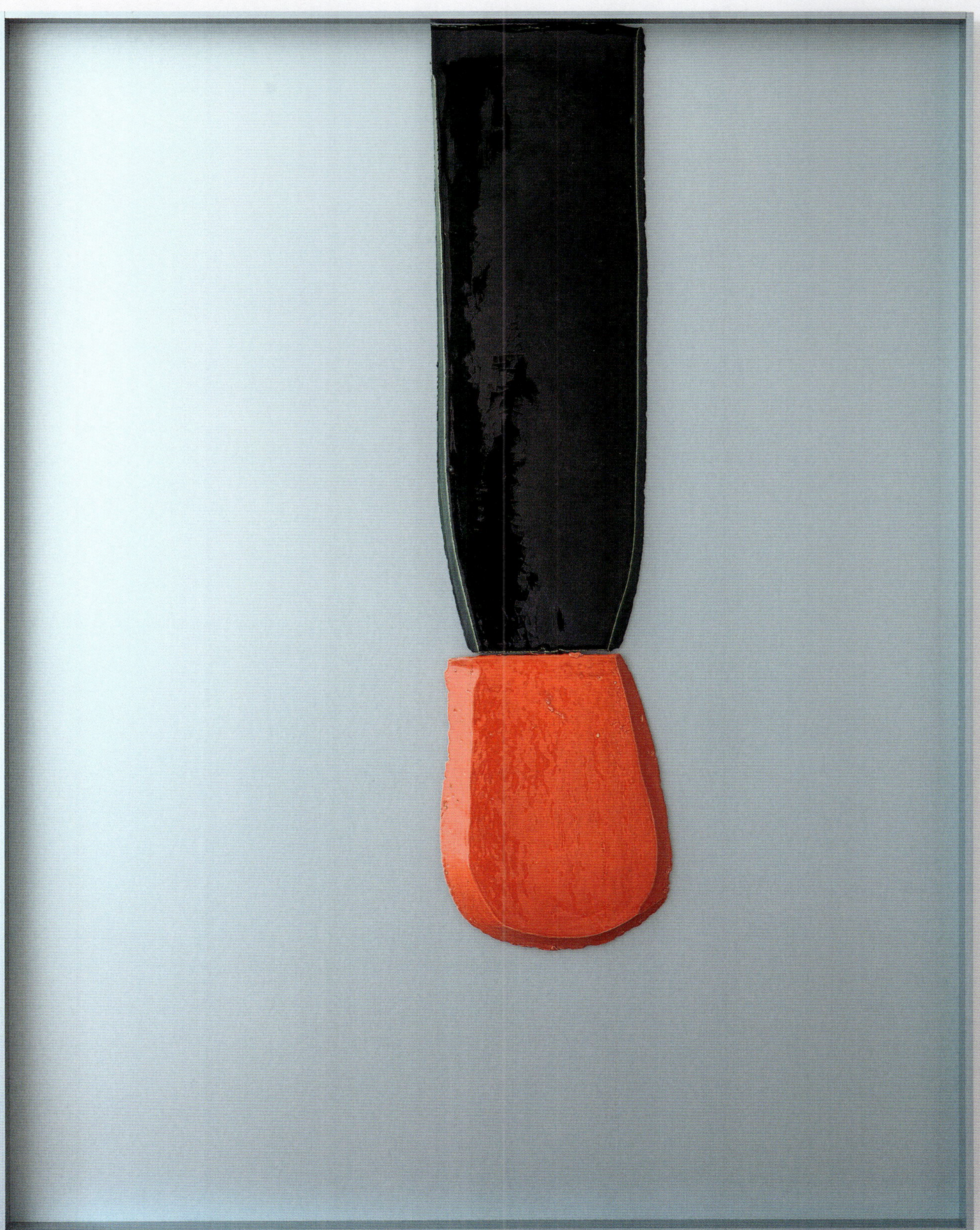

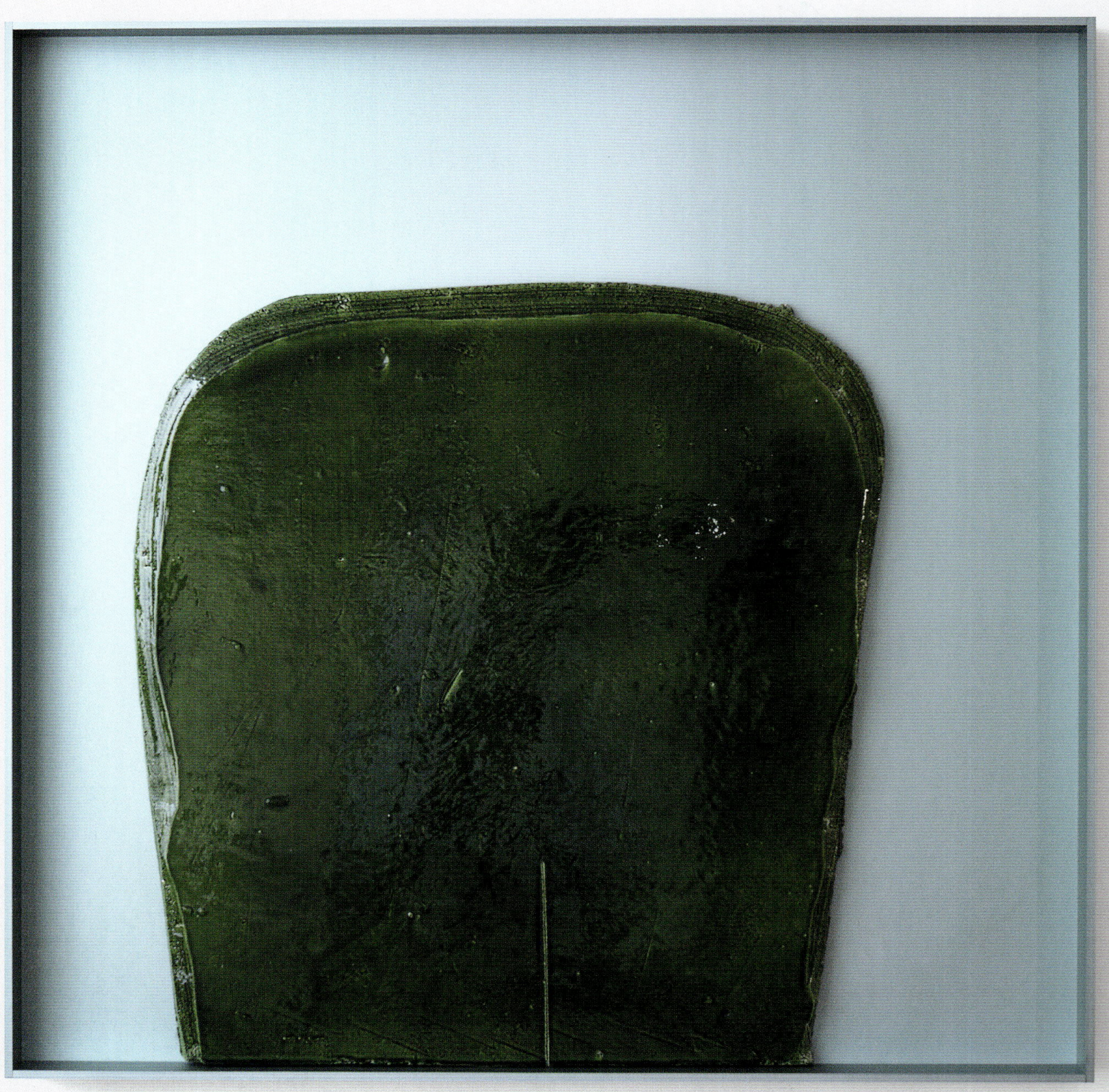

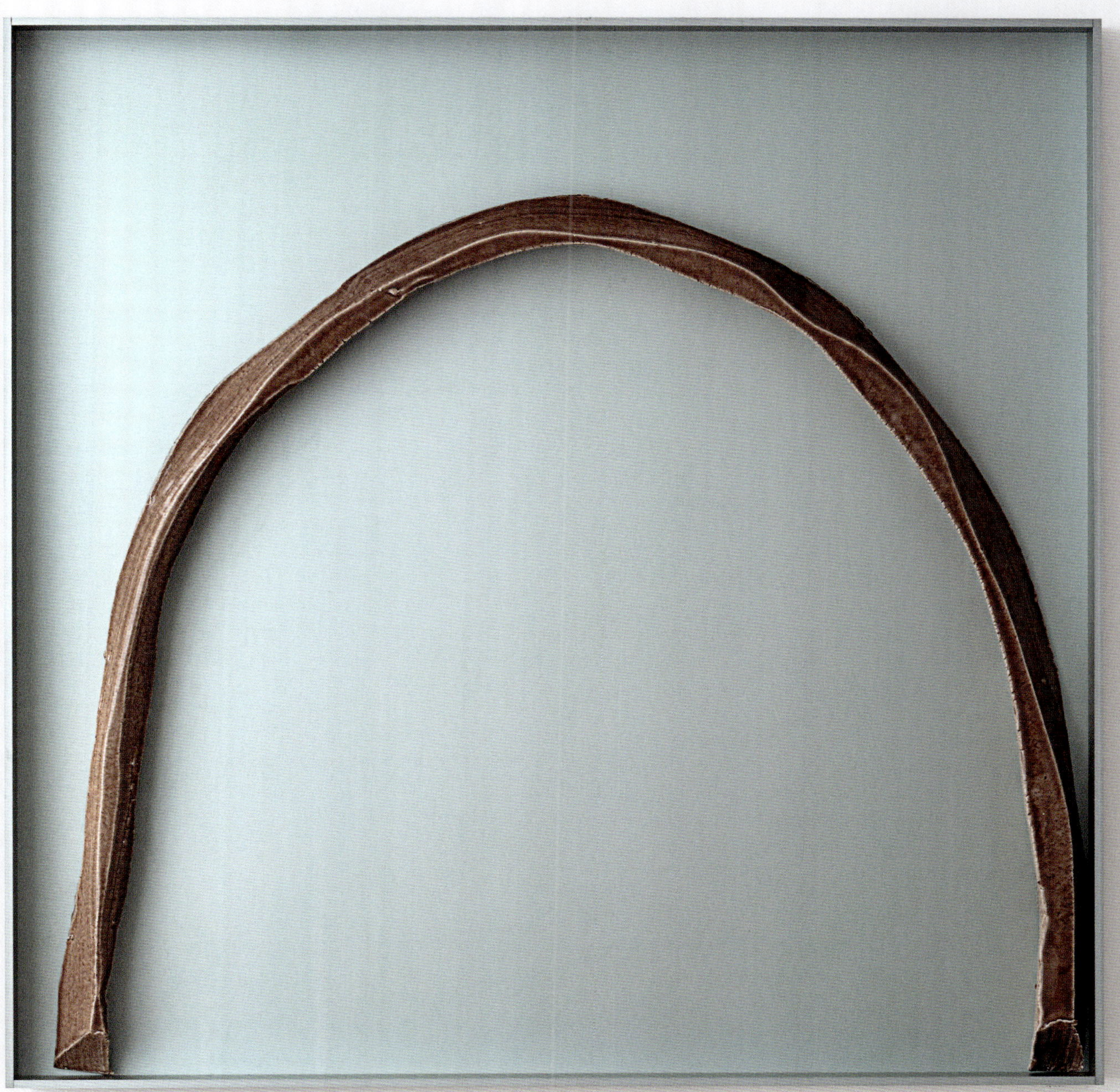

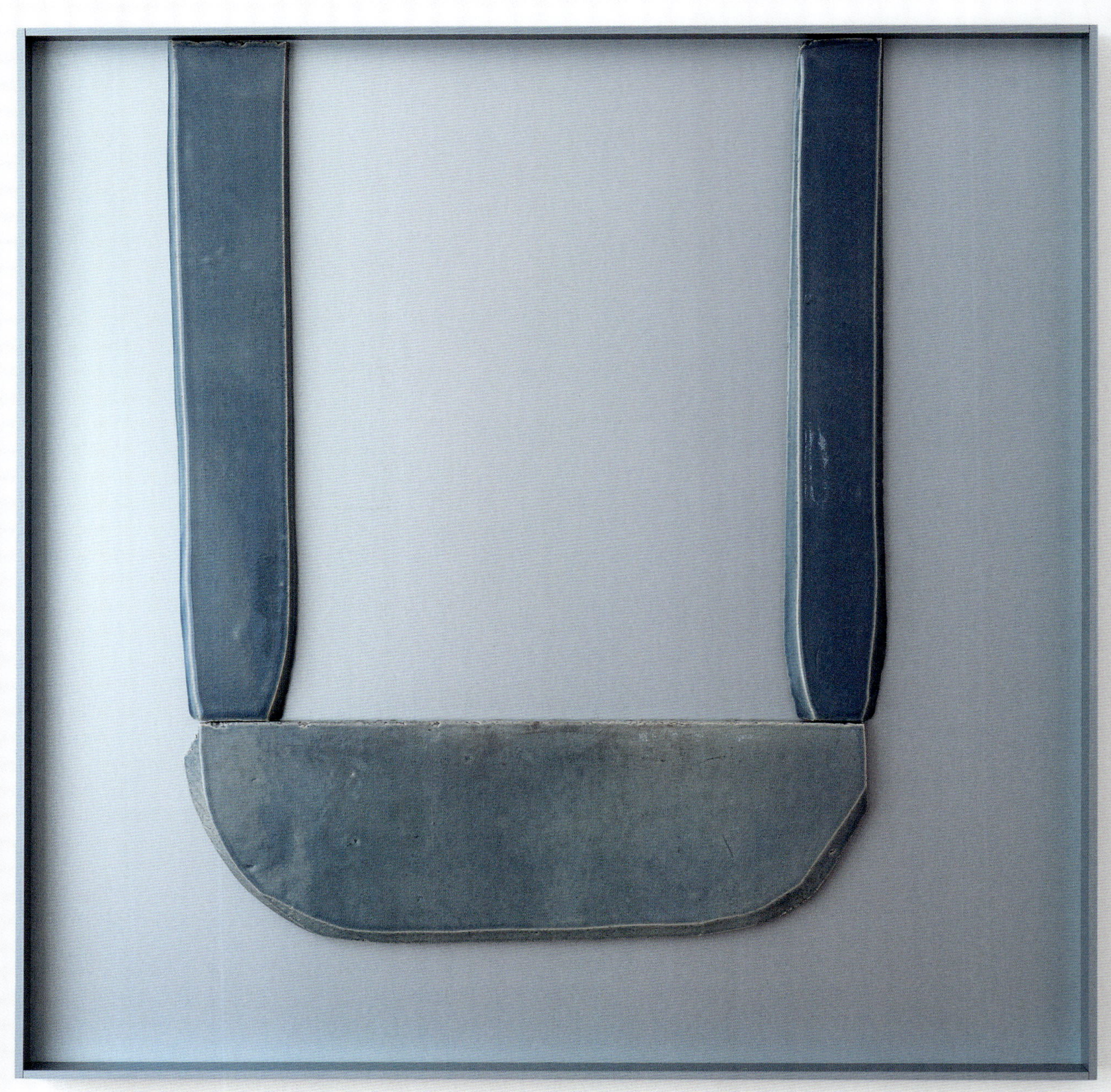

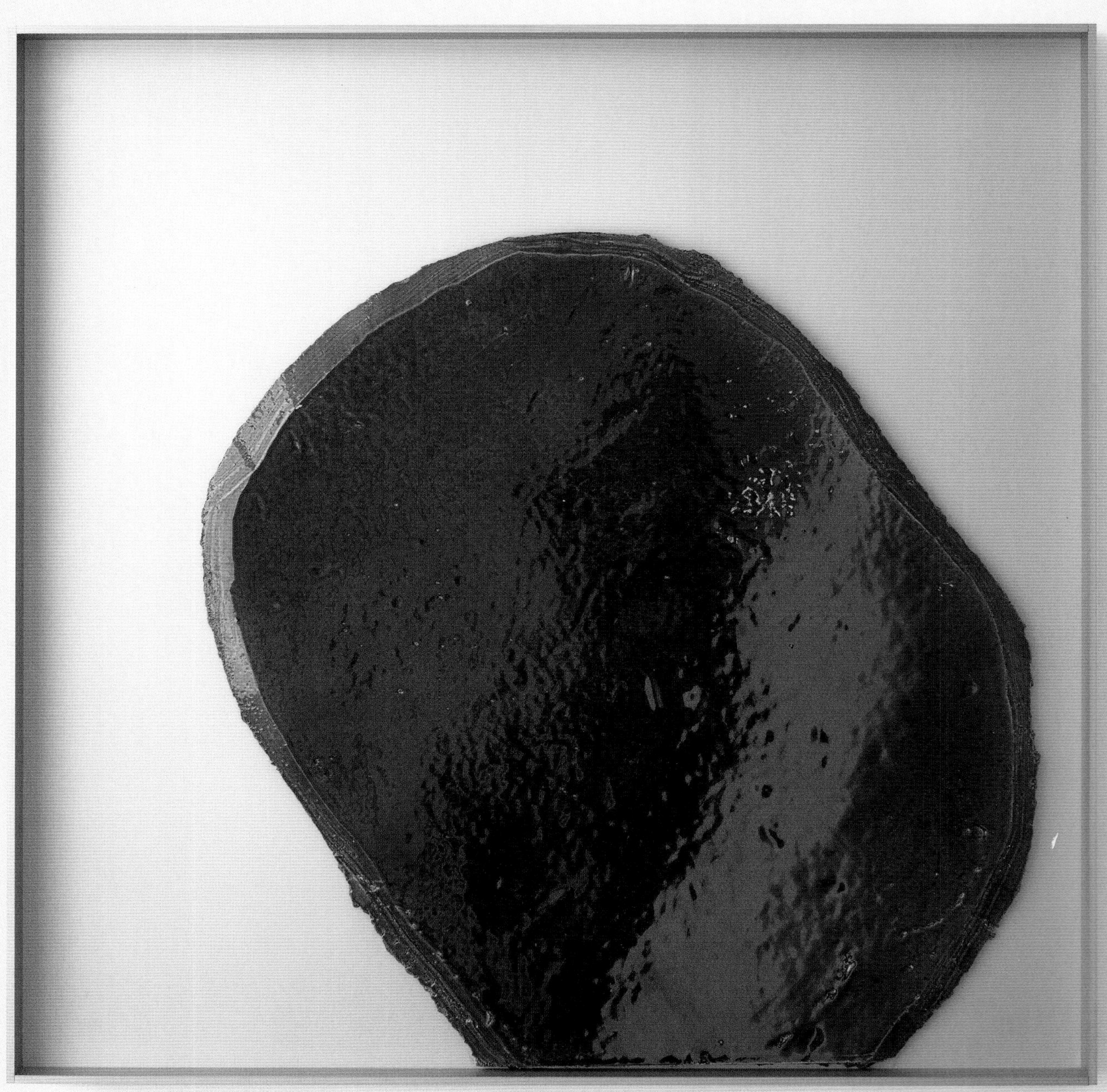

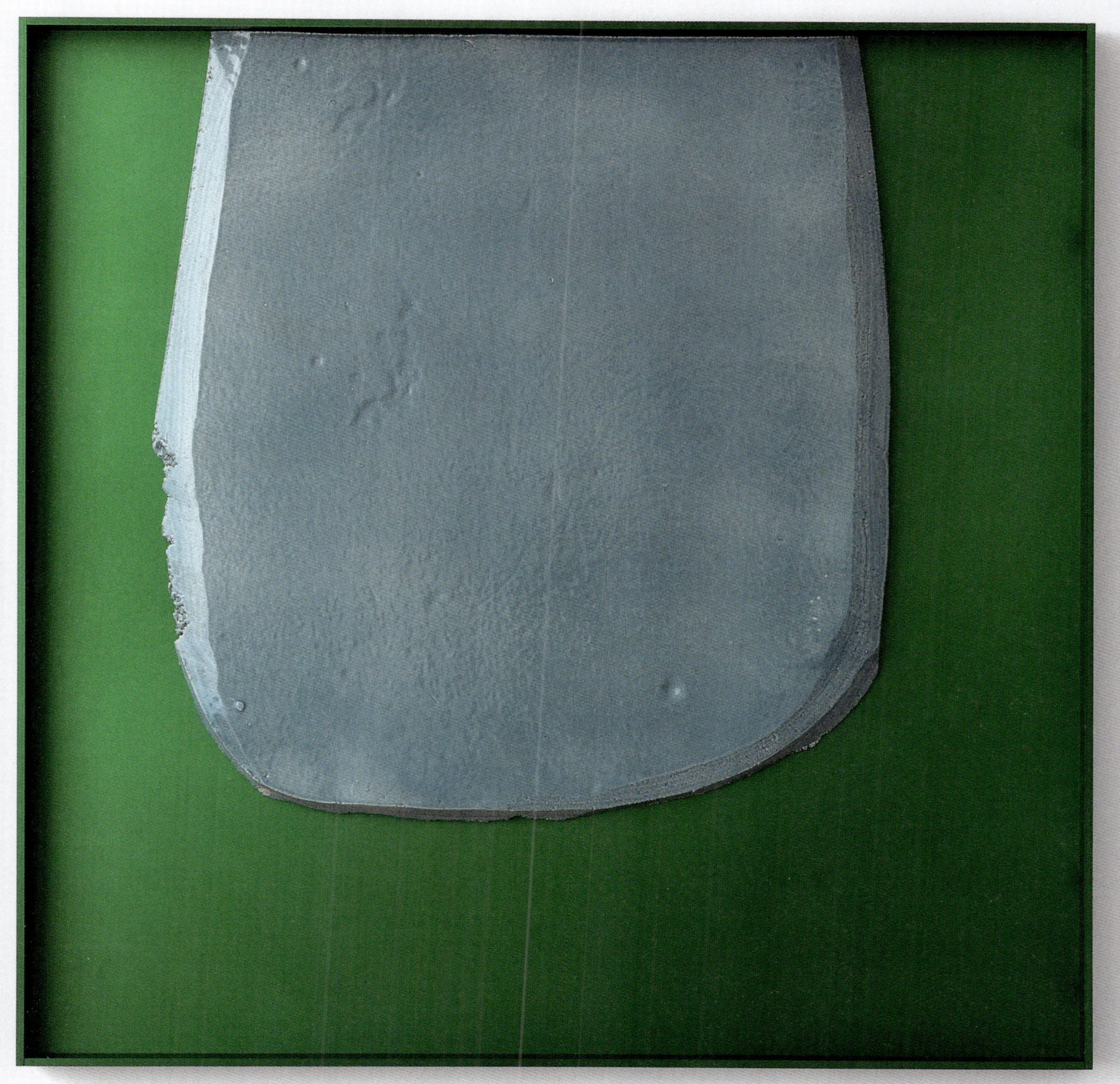

*Bas-Reliefs*
Ronan Bouroullec

First Edition

In collaboration with Galerie kreo
Lithography by Marjeta Morinc

Published by Nieves
www.nievesbooks.com

© 2022 Ronan Bouroullec and Nieves
Reproduction without permission prohibited

ISBN 978-3-907179-44-4